TARANGINI

7

Swami Chinmayananda
and
Swamini Saradapriyananda

CENTRAL CHINMAYA MISSION TRUST

Total no. of copies printed between 1990 to March 2010 - 25,000 copies
Second Edition April 2012 - 3000 copies
Reprint April 2015 to January 2022 - 8,000 copies
Reprint August 2024 - 1,500 copies

Published by:
Chinmaya Prakashan
The Publications Division of
Central Chinmaya Mission Trust
Sandeepany Sadhanalaya
Saki Vihar Road, Mumbai 400072, India
Tel.: +91-22-2803 4900
Email: ccmtpublications@chinmayamission.com
Website: www.chinmayamission.com

Distribution Centre in the USA:
Chinmaya Publications West
560 Bridgetown Pike
Feasterville, PA 19053-7240, USA
Tel.: (215) 396-0390, Fax: (215) 396-9710
Email: publications@chinmayamission.org
Website: www.chinmayapublications.com

Design and Illustrations: Blue Fish

Printed by: Thomson Press (India) Ltd., Faridabad

ISBN: 978-81-7597-526-2

CONTENTS

Listen!
Ye Children
of
Immortal Bliss!

Recommendation

An advertisement once appeared in the newspapers inviting applications for the post of an executive in a very big firm. A number of qualifications and prerequisites had been mentioned for the post and required a man of hard work and integrity.

This country always had an acute unemployment problem. So hundreds of applications arrived. The applicants were all invited for an interview. On the day of the interview, several candidates came with recommendations from highly influential persons. The manager of the firm conducted the interviews. His friend was sitting in one corner of the room, quietly observing the interviews taking place. After all the candidates had been interviewed, the manager selected one of them for the post and immediately sent him an appointment letter.

His friend was very surprised when he saw the selected candidate. He asked the manager,

"My dear friend, this man did not come with any recommendations nor does he have previous experience. Most of the others produced several certificates to prove their experience and efficiency. Why did you select him?"

The manager smiled and said, "He had a better recommendation than the others. They merely produced papers stating that they were efficient, but they could not prove it in their actions. This man did not bring any papers, but actually demonstrated how sincere and efficient he is. So I selected him."

The friend was curious. He asked "What did he do that the others did not? I was sitting here. I did not see him doing anything special."

The manager replied, "I allowed some papers to fly from my table every time a candidate was in the room. None of the candidates bothered

to pick them up. This candidate immediately picked up the papers and put them neatly on the table. He took care to put the paper weight on them so that they did not fly again. The others just came in and went out, either banging the door or not bothering to close it. This man carefully closed the door when he came in and again closed it when he went out. The way he stood and answered my questions showed that he was modest and respectful and not boastful while talking. The others were exactly opposite. They were arrogant and too cocksure of themselves. This is what I personally observed. What need is there for letters of recommendation?"

The friend agreed with the manager's opinion. An ounce of correct behaviour is better than a ton of recommendations.

Then What?

Swami Vivekananda was sailing to America for the second time. He met an Indian student on the ship who was also going to America for higher studies. He looked very sophisticated and behaved arrogantly, as very few people went abroad those days. Swami Vivekananda thought that this would be the right time to give him some lessons in the proper values of life. So one evening, when they met on the deck, Swamiji asked the student, "Son, what are you going to America for?"

"I am going for higher studies, Sir. It will take four to five years."

"Then what will happen?"

"I will return to India. I am sure to get a very good job and earn a lot of money."

"Then?"

"Then?" The student was surprised. Was the Swami so ignorant that he did not know the value of money? "Then Sir, I shall be the most fortunate person. All the fathers of marriageable girls will come to me with proposals. I will be in a position to dictate my own terms and marry the girl of my choice. They will give a substantial dowry too!"

"Then?"

The student felt irritated by these questions, but he did not show it. However, he answered impatiently, "Then Sir, we will live together, and have children. 1 shall be a big officer, with a huge bungalow to live in and a car too. My children will get the best of education, and all opportunities to do well in life. My daughters will make good matches and my sons may even go abroad like me for higher studies and get good jobs."

"Then?"

Now the student was certain that the Swami was mocking him. He looked at his face to see his expression, but the Swami's face was expressionless. So suppressing his mounting irritation, the student replied, "Sir, by the time my children are settled in life, I shall be nearing the age of retirement. So I will build a small house in my village, and live there after retirement. I will get a good pension and manage to live quite comfortably."

"Then?"

The student lost control over himself this time. He retorted angrily, "Then? What sort of questions do you ask, Sir! What more is there to say? Then one day I will die."

The Swami smiled calmly and said, "If it is only to earn, eat, produce children and then one day

die, what is human life worth? Are not the animals doing the same without foreign education? Are not the birds doing the same without schooling? Are not the fish doing the same thing without high salaries and bungalows? Birth and death are common to all beings.

No doubt one should live a decent life, but one should always have high ideals. It is fine to have money and position but they are only worthwhile if used in the service of others."

The student felt duly ashamed and that day onwards resolved to lead a purposeful life in the service of society.

A Mere Dharmashala

Once a sannyasin was standing in front of a king's palace when a stranger to the town came up to him and asked, "Good Sir, what building is this?"

The sannyasin replied, "This is a dharmashala."

At that time the king was standing on one of the balconies of the palace and clearly heard the sannyasin. He was very angry to hear his palace described as a dharmashala. What did he mean, 'a dharmashala'? He immediately sent for the sannyasin and shouted at him, "Don't you have eyes to see? This is my palace. Why did you say that it was a dharmashala? Don't you know the difference?"

The sannyasin innocently asked, "King, what is the difference between a dharmashala and a palace?"

The king shouted again, "A dharmashala is a place where people come, stay for a while and go away. This palace is my place of dwelling."

The sannyasin then asked, "King, when did you come into this palace?"

"I did not come from anywhere. I was born in this palace itself forty five years ago. I shall always stay here and not go anywhere else."

"Before you were born, who dwelt here?"

"My father. He too was born here and lived here for seventy years. He always lived here."

"Before him?"

"My grandfather. He was also born in this very palace and dwelt here for sixty five years. Before him his father, grandfather, and great grandfather dwelt here. For generations we have been here. Now do you know why it is not a dharmashala?"

"King, you have just proved that I am right. Your grandfather came here from somewhere, dwelt for sixty five years and went away. Then your father came from somewhere, dwelt for seventy years and went away. You came forty five years ago and will go away after some time.

Then it will be the turn of your sons and grandsons. All of you are coming and going. So is this palace not a dharmashala?"

The king understood the sannyasin and was ashamed of himself for being angry with him.

Love

Jayadeva was the most famous poet of Orissa, He wrote the Geet Govinda which depicts the eternal love of Radha and Krishna. He was also an accomplished musician, while his wife Padmavati was an exquisite dancer. While she danced he sang the Geet Govinda. They made a perfect pair, complementing each other's talents, and their love was as deep as that of Radha and Krishna.

The king of Orissa had great respect for this couple whose lives were completely dedicated to the Lord.

Once, when Padmavati was with the queen and other ladies of the court, they spoke about a woman who was a great pativrata. When her husband died, she followed him to the cremation ground and burnt herself on his funeral pyre. All the ladies praised her but Padmavati remained silent. The queen then said, "What do you think about this Padmavati?"

Padmavati replied, "Your Majesty, I do not think much of the love of a woman who could live to reach the cremation ground after her husband's death. Will not a real pativrata drop down dead the moment her husband dies?"

The queen and her companions were surprised to hear her speak in such a lofty manner.

Soon after, Padmavati left them and went home. The ladies criticised her and said that she was merely posing to be a great pativrata. The truth would be known when she faced such a situation. One of them said, 'I have an idea. Why don't we send her a false report about the death of her husband and see her reaction?'

They schemed and planned and got their opportunity soon. Jayadeva had accompanied the king on a hunting expedition. They were to be away for two or three days. On the second day of the expedition, the queen asked one of the attendants to bring urgent information, as if from the forest, that Jayadeva had been killed by a lion during the hunt. The queen and other ladies of the court gathered at Padmavati's house to be present when the information came.

As arranged, while everyone sat and talked, a man came in running, appearing to be in great agitation. He stood before Padmavati and started sobbing. The ladies drew near to catch every expression of Padmavati's face. Padmavati looked at the messenger perplexed and asked him what the matter was. In between sobs he told her that Jayadeva had been killed by a lion in the forest and that his body was being brought home soon.

The moment she heard this, Padmavati went pale. She trembled violently till her whole body shook and fell down dead! The queen and her companions rushed forward to catch her and prevent her from falling down. But by that time she was already dead. They were aghast! They never imagined that Padmavati

would really die. Now how would they explain this to Jayadeva? How could they explain her death to the king who had such great love for the couple? There was loud lamentation everywhere and no one knew what to do.

A messenger was sent to the forest to inform the hunting party of Padmavati's passing away. The king and Jayadeva rushed back from the forest. When the king came to know how the plot had been hatched to test Padmavati's devotion to Jayadeva, he was incensed with anger and drew his sword to kill the queen. Jayadeva stopped the king and consoled him saying that it was fate that had made the queen act in such a way. Then he closed his eyes and sincerely prayed to the Lord of his heart, Sri Krishna, "Dear Lord. I have loved Padmavati as much as she loved me. Without her, my life would lose its

meaning. So either restore her to life or take me away."

The Lord said to Jayadeva, "Padmavati's life-span was over. So she died. No one may live beyond his or her allotted years. However, since you have both been so devoted to me, she may live again if you give her half your remaining years on earth. Thus you will both die at one and the same time and be saved the suffering of parting from each other.

Jayadeva prayed that half his life may be transferred to Padmavati. The Lord accordingly blessed them both and Padmavati awoke as if from deep slumber. There was great rejoicing all around.

Such is the power of true love.

A Thief in Hiding

One night a man lying fast asleep in bed was woken up, by a stealthy sound in the room. Still lying in bed, he carefully looked around to see where the noise came from. When his eyes grew accustomed to the darkness, he saw that a thief had quietly entered the bedroom and was hiding in one of the niches. What should he do? He and his wife lived alone in the house and it would not be possible for them to catch the thief by themselves. He could be armed and there might be others with him. The man

did some fast thinking. He woke up his wife and started talking to her. Seeing that the couple was awake, the thief remained in hiding and listened to their conversation.

The husband told his wife loudly, "Dear, do you know, I had a very nice dream? I dreamt that by God's grace, a bonny boy was born to us."

"Really?" said the overjoyed wife. "Wouldn't it be lovely to have a child after so many years? I think we should go on a pilgrimage."

"Sure," said the husband. "But when the boy is born, what should we call him?"

"We don't know whether we will have any more sons. So we should include the names of all our people so that no one will be offended later on."

"Yes, you are right, my father's name, your father's name..."

Before the husband finished, the wife joined in enthusiastically, "Our family diety's name, and Guru's name..."

"Remember, we should be grateful to one more person and add his name too at the end," added the husband.

"Who is that?" asked the wife.

The husband replied, "Don't you know that we are protected every night by the night watchman, Rama?"

"Yes, yes," the wife agreed. "We should remember him too. Let us add his name at the end."

"Rama is a nice ending to a long name. In any case we can't call him by a long name every time. We can just call him Rama. It is a beautiful name, don't you think so?"

His wife agreed heartily. The thief could clearly hear the conversation between husband and wife. He was highly amused at their serious discussion about the name of a boy who was not even yet conceived. He chuckled to himself as the dialogue continued.

"Suppose our boy grows up and plays with toys in the hall while you are busy in the kitchen, how will you call him?"

"Where is the difficulty? I shall say, 'Rama, Rama, come here.' My voice can easily be heard in the hall from the kitchen."

"Sure," added the husband. "He can hear it if he is in the hall. But suppose he is out on the road playing with other children, he will not hear you."

"Then I will go on to the balcony and call him aloud." So saying, she got up from the bed, went to the balcony and actually cried out, "Rama, Rama, come here at once." Then she came back and asked her husband, "My voice will then be heard, won't it?"

"Yes, it will be, if he is playing on this road," agreed the husband. "But if he happens to be playing in the next street, then this voice won't do."

His wife once again went to the balcony and cried out in a loud voice, "Rama, Rama, come here at once... O Rama, Rama, come here at once." Then she turned back and asked, "I was loud enough to be heard by the entire neighbourhood, wasn't I?"

She was. Hearing her cry, the night watchman Rama, who was in the next street, came running to see why he had been called! He came and knocked their door. The husband smiled inwardly, for his plan had worked. He got up as though naturally, and unlocked the front door.

Rama, the watchman asked, "What is the matter? Why did you call me?"

The husband replied, "Please excuse us. We didn't mean to call you. We were calling our son in the next street. If you have any doubt, please ask the gentleman hiding in the niche. He has listened to our conversation right from the beginning."

So saying he pointed to the thief comfortably settled in the niche. The thief had been so engrossed in following this unusual dialogue that he was caught unaware. The watchman nabbed him there and then and led him to jail.

If you keep cool in an emergency, the Lord will show you a way out!

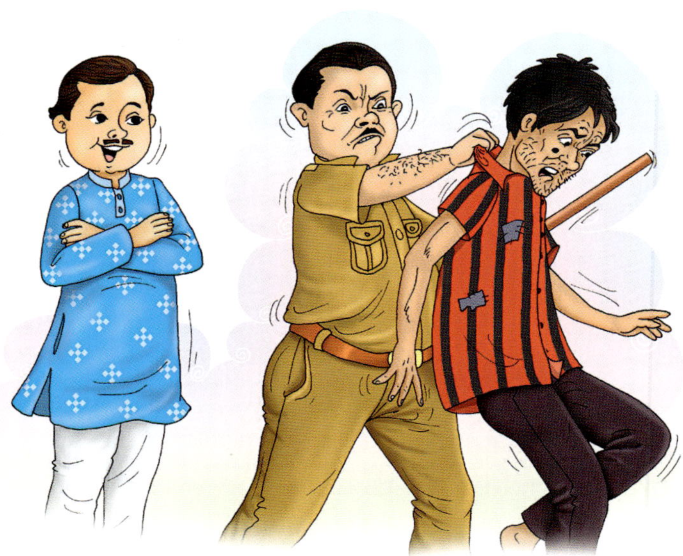

A Man's Dilemma

Before attaining mahanirvana, the Buddha, we are told, had five hundred earlier births. In each of these he performed austerities and lived a righteous life. In one of these lives, he was born as a wise Master and gave right advice to all, those who came to him, to guide them on the spiritual path.

One day, a strange incident occurred. One man had gone from his own village to another on an urgent matter. His wife packed some food for his lunch and dinner. He kept the food packet in a cloth bag which he tied in a loose knot and placed it on his head.

At lunch time he happened to pass through a dense forest. Tired by the hours of walking, he ate the food and fell asleep.

While he slept, a cobra slithered around and entered the bag containing the food packet. It lay there, comfortably coiled. When the man awoke, without suspecting the presence of the cobra, he picked up his bag put it on his head and walked on.

On reaching his destination, he finished his work and in the evening was returning to his village. In another three hours he would be home!

On the way back he met a soothsayer. The soothsayer looked at him and said, "Sir, if you spend the night in some place other than your home, you will die. On the other hand, if you reach home tonight, your wife will die!" The man was troubled. He wanted to live but he loved his wife dearly and did not wish to cause her death. Now what should he do? Go home and cause her death or remain away and invite death for himself? It was a difficult decision to make and he urgently needed advice.

Suddenly he remembered the wise Master, who

was camping in a village nearby. He decided to go to the Master with his problem and seek his advice.

When he reached the village, he found the Master surrounded by people gathered for satsanga. He prostrated to the Master and told him of his dilemma. The Master looked at him lovingly. When he had finished narrating his story the Master asked him, "If you stay away from home for the night, what will you do for food?"

The man said, "There is food in my bag, Master. I will eat it and sleep under a tree."

The Master asked again, "Suppose you go home for the night, what will you eat then?"

The man replied, "My wife will give me the food she cooks in the evening and will herself eat the food in the bag."

The Master looked thoughtfully at the bag lying on the ground and detected the crawling movement of the cobra inside. Then he said, "My dear man, what the soothsayer said, is correct. Look in your bag carefully. There is a live cobra inside it. If you had stopped on the way, you would have opened it to eat your food.

The cobra would have bitten you and caused your death. If you had gone home for the night, your wife would have opened the bag and been bitten by the cobra. Then, she would have died. Now

that you know the reason, neither of you need die. Kill the vicious serpent and save yourself."

The man followed the Master's advice and went home happily.

We all have the serpent of anger, greed and jealousy in the bag of our mind. The Master tells us about its existence. If, according to his advice, we kill it, we will be able to live happily in this world.

The Coconuts And The Boons

Once upon a time, a priest and a merchant together performed austerities for a long time to propitiate Lord Shiva. At last the Lord pleased with their tapas, gave them darshan. He presented three coconuts to the priest and one to the merchant and said, 'Now return to your respective homes along with the coconuts. After performing puja, you may wish for anything you want. Then break the coconuts. Your wishes will come true.'

The priest was very happy that he had more coconuts than the merchant. The merchant was intelligent and not perturbed at having got only one coconut. He went home cheerfully. The priest too went home, sailing on winds of wishful thinking, planning out all the things he would wish for, before breaking each coconut.

When he reached home, he performed the puja as instructed by the Lord. He was about to wish for something and had lifted up the coconut to break it. Exactly at that moment, his wife spoke from behind, "Since you have three coconuts, please get what you want with two of them. With the third one, please wish that my people should become rich." The priest became very angry with his wife for making such a demand. He shouted at her, "Riches for your people! My foot!" The last words were still ringing in his ears when the whole house was filled with human feet resembling the priest's foot. His words had literally come true. There was no place to move about. Thousands and thousands of feet lay everywhere. Both husband and wife were horrified. The wife cried out, "How many feet have you got? How are you going to live with all these feet hanging from you? Please break the second coconut wishing for all these feet to go away." The poor priest could think of no other way. He took up the coconut and broke it wishing that the feet should go away. The moment the coconut broke, his wish came true. All the feet vanished including his original two feet! Now he lay there, a torso without even the stumps of his legs. What was he to do? He lifted up the third coconut and broke it wishing that his original legs should be restored. All the three

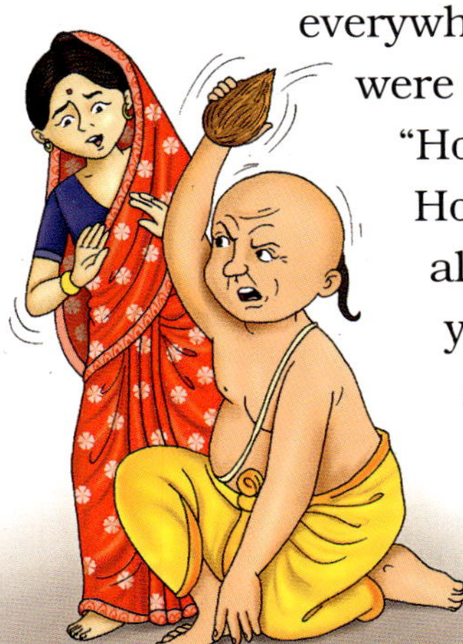

coconuts were gone and the priest remained as poor as before.

The merchant on the other hand went home, calmly discussed with his wife what they wanted best and after puja broke the coconut wishing, 'In time, my wife and I should lay our great grandson in a golden cradle on the fourth floor of our own house, while all our relatives alongwith our sons, grandsons and their wives witness the ceremony.'

In time his wish, too, came true.

None of us lacks good luck. We only lack good sense and like the foolish priest we lose the opportunities that come to us time and time again.

A Mahatma's Blessing

Once upon a time, there was a devout man who had no children. He visited several sacred places, worshipped in famous temples, but remained childless. One day he met the sage Narada who was wandering around the world. He begged Narada to find out from Brahmaji, the creator, whether he would have any children in this life. Narada blessed him and promised to do so.

When Narada went to Brahmaloka, he spoke to his father Lord Brahma about the man. Brahmaji said, "Narada, this man will not have any children in this life because according to his prarabdha he does not deserve any children. Narada was sorry for the man but one cannot escape one's prarabdha and he could not do anything about it. A few years passed. Narada was again on his rounds of the world. As it happened, he passed the same man's house. Narada remembered his promise to the man. He decided to go in and tell him that he would not have children in this life.

Even as he was thinking of going in and meeting the man, three children, all chubby and healthy, came running out of the house, laughing and chasing each other. Behind them came the man himself laughing along with the children. The moment he came out, he saw and recognised Narada. He came forward and prostrated to him and called the children to do likewise. Shyly the children came and prostrated before the sage. Narada blessed

them and asked the man whose children they were. He replied, "O sage, these children are mine."

Narada was surprised! Brahmaji had said

that this man would not have any children in this life. How then did he beget them? Was his father, the creator of the whole universe, wrong? He went straight to Brahmaloka once again. Brahmaji was surprised to see Narada. Narada said, "Father, you told me that this man would have no children in this life. I am just coming from his house. He has three children now. How did your rules of creation go wrong?"

Brahmaji smiled at him and said, "True, as per his prarabdha he should not have had any children. But he was blessed by a great Mahatma. When a Mahatma gives his blessings, even prarabdha is pushed aside!"

Devotion To The Guru

In olden days, from a very young age, children stayed in the ashramas of their Gurus to study. They were treated as members of the Guru's family. The boys served their teacher and his wife with great love and implicit obedience. To test their devotion the teacher used to set them varied tasks, sometimes even very difficult ones.

Once a student called Upamanyu was serving his teacher Dhaumya. The boy was a newcomer and the teacher was watching him carefully. In those days, it was the custom for the students in a gurukula to beg for alms and bring them to the teacher.

One day, Dhaumya asked Upamanyu, "Son, how are you feeding yourself?"

The boy said respectfully, "Sir, I beg from householders and eat the alms."

The teacher feigned surprise. “Don’t you know, my dear, that whatever alms you get must be offered to your teacher? From tomorrow, bring to me the bhiksha that you get.”

From that day onwards, Upamanyu offered the alms to the teacher who kept it all for himself without giving anything to the student.

The student did not protest. The teacher was secretly observing Upamanyu. Ten days passed in this manner. Upamanyu looked neither famished nor weak.

Once again Dhaumya asked him, “Son, how are you living now?”

Upamanyu looked at the teacher with great respect and said, “Sir, I offer you the alms obtained in the first round. I go for a second round and collect food for myself.

Dhaumya looked horrified. "Going a second time?" he exclaimed. "No, son, brahmacharis should not trouble householders twice a day. Stop going a second time."

Following the Guru's instructions, the student stopped going for alms a second time. Dhaumya watched him closely. Another ten days passed. Upamanyu made no protest, nor did he look famished or starved.

Dhaumya once again asked, "Son, how are you being fed?"

The student looked at the teacher with veneration and said, "Sir, after the calves have had their milk from the cows, there is still some milk left. I milk the cows and drink the milk."

The teacher said, "No, son, you should not do that. The cows are very sensitive. If they come to know that you require the milk, out of love for you they will stop feeding their calves. It will be a cruelty to the young ones. Don't do that."

The student bowed his head.

Again a fortnight passed. Dhaumya was quietly watching Upamanyu's reaction. The student was, as usual diligent, active and obedient. He didn't look starved or weak.

Dhaumya asked, "Son, what are you eating these days?"

Upamanyu replied with great humility, "Sir, when the calves feed from their mothers, often some milk comes out as foam from their mouths. I collect the foam and swallow it."

The teacher looked reproachfully at him and said, "Don't you know that once the calves know that you depend upon the foam for your food they will not feed properly but give out everything as foam and starve? It will be a great cruelty to them. Don't do it any more" Upamanyu promised not to repeat it again.

That day onwards, Upamanyu started becoming lean and weak. He was so starved he could move about only with great difficulty. Still he attended to all his duties without either protesting or making an excuse. With growing admiration, Dhaumya watched his student. Ten days passed. Upamanyu was reduced to skin and bones. When he walked he looked like a grass reed swaying in the wind. Still he carried on. On the tenth day, he took the cattle into the forest for grazing. Being starved for ten days, he could not withstand his hunger anymore. He plucked some leaves from the trees and ate them. One of the trees was poisonous. When he ate the poisonous leaves he became totally blind and could not see anything. Groping about with unseeing eyes, he staggered and fell into an old well. He could see nothing and so did not know how to come out of it.

When evening came, the cattle found their way back to the ashrama but the boy was missing. Dhaumya knew something must have happened to him. It was already dark, so Dhaumya set out with a lighted torch. He went into the forest loudly calling out to Upamanyu. As the teacher came near the well, Upamanyu heard him and cried out, "Sir, I am here in the well."

The teacher came near the well and peeped in. "How did you fall into the well, son?" he asked.

Upamanyu explained how he had become blind by eating some leaves and how he had stumbled into the well.

Dhaumya taught him a mantra to invoke the Asvinikumaras, the divine physicians.

Upamanyu repeated the mantra with intense

devotion. The Asvinikumaras appeared before him with a bowl containing kheer. They asked him to eat it saying his sight would be restored to him.

But Upamanyu said, "O divine Sirs. I cannot eat this kheera. All good that I get should be offered to the teacher. I request you to offer it to my teacher."

The Asvinikumaras were pleased with his gurubhakti. They restored his eyesight, lifted him out of the well and left him with Dhaumya. Upamanyu prostrated to his teacher with great reverence. Dhaumya blessed him and embraced him with affection. By the grace of the teacher, Upamanyu became adept in all the sciences and came to be regarded by all as the example of an ideal student.

Timmarusu

Timmarusu was the renowned minister of the Emperor Sri Krishna Devaraya of the Vijayanagaram empire. He was wise and astute but had humble beginnings. This is the story of how he rose to become a trusted minister.

There was an old minister of the Vijayanagaram Emperor who had faithfully served his master. He was becoming old and feeble and was unable to attend to the affairs of the kingdom as before. He wanted to select an intelligent man as his successor while he was still alive so that he could suitably train the minister elect. To find out who was the most intelligent man in the kingdom, he drew a long straight line on a piece of paper and sent it around the kingdom. Anyone who could make the straight line smaller without erasing any part of it would be the new minister.

The king's attendants who carried the paper from place to place were instructed to show it to each and every person, irrespective of age, caste, creed and status in life.

They travelled far and wide. Everyone who saw the line despaired. How could anyone make it shorter, without erasing any part of it? One day, the attendants reached a small village and took the paper to the village school and explained to the school teacher what was to be done.

The teacher shook his head and said that it was impossible.

Then the attendants said, "Allow us to show the paper to the students also. They may have an answer."

The teacher smiled. If he, the teacher, could not find a solution, how could the young boys do it? Anyway, the problem was put before the students.

Timmarusu was one of the pupils of the school. He got up immediately and said, "Sir, I can do it."

The attendants stared at him in disbelief. "You!" laughed the teacher, "All right, come on, let us see what you can do."

The boy came forward, picked up a pencil and drew a straight line by the side of the original line on the paper. He drew his line much longer, projecting beyond the original line at both ends. Sure enough, by the side of the new line, the original line was shorter! The teacher and the attendants applauded his great commonsense. What a simple way of making the line smaller!

Timmarusu was at once selected to be the future minister. He fulfilled all the hopes of his political teacher and rose in life to become one of the most famous ministers ever.

Keep A Cool Head

One evening, a farmer returned from his field dusty and tired. As usual, his wife had kept two buckets of water in the backyard for his bath. As the farmer sat on the stool and took a mug full of water from the bucket, he noticed that someone was crouching behind the bushes. Perhaps a thief! He must be waiting there for nightfall so that he could loot the house and run away in the darkness. Now how was he to catch him? The farmer and his wife were alone in the house. By themselves they would not be able to catch him. The farmer thought quickly and planned his course of action.

Instead of taking a bath as usual, he poured the water in his mouth and then spat it out onto the bushes where the thief was hiding. Again and again he took mouthsful of water and spat it out. The thief sat silently behind the bushes and suffered because he did not want to be caught.

In this way two buckets of water were exhausted. The farmer cried out to his wife for more water. She wondered why he wanted more water that day. Nevertheless, she brought him two more buckets of water.

Again the farmer spat out the whole lot and asked for more. His wife patiently brought more water four or five times, but when he demanded some more a sixth time she lost her patience and shouted at him, 'What is wrong with you today? You have not even started your bath. All you do is spit out mouthful of water. What is the meaning of this?'

So the husband spat out the water at her. Now she was sure that he had suddenly become mad. She cried out aloud to her neighbours, 'Please come and save me. My husband has suddenly turned mad.'

Hearing her cries all the neighbours came running and asked the farmer what the matter was. The farmer complained in an indignant voice. 'Sirs, look at this ungrateful wife of mine. I feed her, clothe her and give her ornaments. I have spat water at her just once and she raises her voice and calls me mad. Look at the gentleman in the bushes. He is an utter stranger to me. He has sat quietly without complaining even though I have spat out ten buckets of water at him!'

All those gathered there saw the thief in the bushes. They caught him and took him to jail. The farmer's wife and his neighbours congratulated him for his presence of mind and quick thinking.

If you keep a cool head, you can think your way out of the trickiest situations in life.

Tyagaraja

Tyagaraja was devoted to Lord Rama from his very childhood. As he grew up, his fervour grew deeper and deeper. He withdrew from all mundane work and devoted himself to the worship of the Lord. He was an extraordinarily talented musician too. So throughout the day he would spend his time singing and worshipping his beloved Lord.

Tyagaraja's elder brother and his wife were the opposite of Tyagaraja and his wife. They did not like his seemingly senseless worship. They thought that he just whiled away his precious time without earning and acquiring money. They abused Tyagaraja, created as many obstacles as possible in his worship, and finally told him to leave their house and live separately. The family house was partitioned and Tyagaraja and his wife went to live elsewhere. Since both husband and wife were of one mind in their devotion to the Lord, they spent all their time in worship with no thought for their material poverty.

Their devotion and saintly life attracted many people and soon, by Sri Rama's grace, all their material needs were fulfilled by themselves. Their house became as good as a temple and there was a continuous flow of devotees and wealth. The couple lived joyously in the company of like-minded people, making use of the barest minimum for their personal needs and giving away everything else to others. Tyagaraja's popularity and prosperity made his brother and his wife very jealous.

One night, when everyone was asleep, Tyagaraja's brother entered his house. He stealthily took the idol of Sri Rama and made straight for the river. He threw the idol into the middle of the river and went back home. The next morning, when Tyagaraja woke, he was distraught with sorrow at the theft. He did not know who had stolen the idol and why. He felt forlorn without his beloved Lord. He wandered from place to place, and even went on a pilgrimage to try and calm his grief.

As he wandered from place to place visiting famous kshetras, Sri Ramanavami approached. About that time Sri Rama appeared to him in a dream and told him to return home by Sri Ramanavami. So, Tyagaraja started his long journey home. He came to the river Kaveri which he had to cross in order to reach his village. The river was angry and in spate. The flood was so violent that no boatman was prepared to risk his boat in the current. The people with Tyagaraja suggested that they wait till the flood abated. Sri Ramanavami was the next day, so how could Tyagaraja afford to wait?

He smiled and said, 'Dear Lord, first you order me to return home and then you create floods before me. Is this your test? Then let me not fail it.' So saying he raised both hands in salutation to Sri Rama and repeating Ramanama, entered the water. The people gathered there were aghast. They cried out in fear, 'Sir, don't be foolish. You will be washed away!'

But there was no turning back for the saint. He could not think of anything but his beloved Sri Rama. With his entire mind fixed on the Lord he went deeper and deeper into the waters while no one could shake either his resolve or his determination. He moved resolutely towards the other shore where several people had gathered to watch with wonderment the approaching figure of Tyagaraja.

Suddenly from out of the waters rose the idol which had been thrown into the river many months ago. Tyagaraja was already chest deep in water when he saw it. Gladness and joy filled his heart! 'My Rama, have you too walked here to reach me?' He burst into song in midstream, clasping his beloved Lord to his bosom.

Tyagaraja then came out of the waters and went home. His wife, too, was doubly pleased with the return of her husband and of the Lord. Understandably, that year's Sri Ramanavami was the most joyous of all their celebrations!

Sri Krishna Tulabhara

(In Dwaraka, Satyabhama's palace. Satyabhama is attending to the decorations in the hall. A maid enters with a basket of flowers and keeps it near Satyabhama).

Satya: Suhasini, do you know where Lord Krishna is?

Suha: Maharani, last night he was with Devi Jambavati. He may be about to leave now.

Satya: Hurry up then and go there. Bow to him on my behalf and submit.... I am planning to have special decorations here tonight. Ask him whether he will come here and see the decorations before he retires for the night.

(Suha bows and goes out)

Satya: *(turning aside)* Madanika! *(another maid enters and bows)* Are the lamps and flowers ready for the special function in the evening?

Madanika: Yes, Maharani.

Satya: The musicians and players?

Mada: They have already arrived.

Satya: Rangasthala decorations?

Mada: They are going on. They will be finished in another two hours.

Satya: Good. You may go now. *(maid bows and leaves, Suha returns and bows).*

Satya: Ah! you have come back! Did you meet Lord Krishna?

Suha: Yes. The Lord was just leaving when I met him. As soon as he saw me, the Lord asked about you.

Satya: *(looking happy)* Did he? What did he say to my message?

Suha: He was planning to spend the whole day at Devi Mitravinda's palace. But when he heard your message, he smiled and said, 'Please inform Satya that her merest wish is my command. I will come there by dusk and will see the decorations.'

Satya: *(happy beyond words).* Did he say that?

Really? He said that my merest wish was his command? He promised to come here, changing his programme, because I expressed my wish! Oh! how lucky I am! I am sure he does not oblige any other person like this. With a smile from my lips, I can make the Lord obey my will! With the threat of a frown from my brows, the Lord hastens to pacify me!

I am the only one who can command the Lord in this way! *(gets up and dances in glee).*

Maids: (they gather as she dances). Oh, Maharani, no one is as lucky as you are. You are dearest to the Lord out of the sixteen thousand wives he has! And we are lucky to be your maids. Because of you we get to see the Lord so frequently.

Satya: Yes. why you alone? Everyone connected with this palace is indeed blessed, because they are all caressed and blessed by the Lord. The Lord likes everything liked by me!

(Narada enters singing. Satybhama prostrates and offers a seat to the sage and offers flowers at his feet. The sage picks up one of the flowers and smells it).

Narada: Ah! what a fragrance! This is the Parijata brought by Krishna from heaven, isn't it?

Satya: *(Proudly smiling).* Yes, you know Divine sage, how the Lord and I had to fight Indra before getting it.

Narada: *(Smiling).* Yes, Satyabhama, Krishna loves you the most of all his wives. Still you have to share the Lord with all of them, you know! But if you are interested there is one vrata by which you can make the Lord all yours.

Satya: *(Eyes sparkling at the thought)* Really? I have not heard of such a vrata so far, Devarshi.

What is the vrata called? How is it to be performed? I am very anxious to perform it and make the Lord

all my own. Please advise me how to do it. *(Joins her palms and looks at him beseechingly).*

Narada: The vrata is called patidana vrata. The vrata itself is simple. It consists of the worship of Mangala Gauri. But the speciality of the vrata is in what follows next. After the puja. you have to gift away your husband to a wise master and then purchase him back by offering something which is equal to his weight. By this vrata the Lord becomes solely yours and you won't have to compete with Rukmini and others.

Satya: When should the vrata be performed. Who will take the gift of the Lord? Please tell me all the details.

Narada: *(Closing his eyes for a second).* Yes, the day after the full moon is best suited for the vrata. The puja is to be done in the morning and followed immediately by the patidana. Before the evening is over you can offer the price and get your husband back. Any wise man can be chosen to receive the gift.

Satya: Sage, who is wiser than you? Please accept the gift of the Lord and oblige me.

Narada: Sure, sure. I have no objection to do you a good turn. But first of all obtain Krishna's consent.

You know, without his approval the gift cannot be made.

Satya: *(Proudly).* Oh, the consent won't take long! I have only to mention it to him. I will make all the preparations for the puja. Please bless me that I may benefit by the vrata.

Narada: *(With a mischievous twinkle).* You will surely benefit much by the vrata.

(Curtain comes down)

(Scene Two)

(The same scene. Narada and Krishna are seated. Satyabhama stands near Krishna. She looks as if she has just finished the vrata with the sacred thread round the wrist.)

Satya: *(Joining her palms)* Divine sage, tell me what is to be done now. I have finished the puja as directed by you.

Narada: Now gift away your husband renouncing all your rights on him.

Satya: Madanika, bring water. *(Madanika brings water in a golden vessel with a spout. Devarshi Narada holds his two palms together upward and Satya pours water into the palms)* Devarshi, I hereby gift away my Lord and husband Krishna, to you. All my rights and claims on him are renounced in your favour. He is no more mine, but yours.

Narada: Now the vrata has been completed in the proper manner. Let us move on. *(Gets up).*

(Krishna also gets up and follows Narada).

Satya: *(Looks at Krishna in surprise)* You are going already? Have you forgotten that you are spending the day with me?

Krishna: *(Looking more surprised)* Yes, but that was fixed when I belonged to you. Now that you have given me away, I have to be with my master who owns me. Good bye.

Satya: *(In consternation, to Narada)* Devarshi, you are taking my husband away?

Narada: *(Lifting his eyebrows)* Sure. I am going now. He will have to come with me. Where else can he be except with me?

Satya: But, Devarshi, you said that 1 can take him back paying something equal to his weight, didn't you?

Narada: True, you may do so before this day is over. Arrange for it and take him back. Anything equal to his weight is to be given. So get a balance ready and arrange for the things. As soon as you are ready, send word to me. In the meanwhile we will be visiting places in Dwaraka. Come, Krishna. This is too heavy for me. You carry it. *(Hands over his tambura to Krishna who takes it dutifully).*

Satya: *(In tears)* O Devarshi, please don't give such menial work to my Lord. *(To Krishna)* Why do you carry his tambura?

Krishna: *(Looking miserable).* Don't you see, my dear, that I am helpless? You have given me away to him. How can I refuse to obey my master?

Satya: *(Entreating Narada)* Divine sage, please don't give such work to my husband. I shall send my servants to carry your things.

Narada: *(Shaking his head)* How can I afford to take your servants with me? I am a poor man. I can't afford to feed them. Even this Krishna will be too expensive for me to keep. I am going straight to the market now. I shall dispose him off by giving him away to the first bidder so that I will be free once again.

Satya: *(Cries out in agony)* O Sage, you are not going to sell my husband to someone else?

Narada: *(Talking to her patiently as if to a child)* Rani Satyabhama, what can be sold to me can be sold to others also. The highest bidder and the first one will get Krishna. If you wish to be the first, you are welcome. Otherwise, even after I sell him, you can repurchase him from the buyer, provided the buyer is willing to sell him. Now it is getting late. Come Krishna. I have to get a good price for you.

(Turning aside and addressing the public)

O' people, listen, here is a unique auction! Hear, hear, hear me all! Here is a unique One to gain; if you are eager to get for a price, One who is priceless: If you are a lover of things beautiful, here is the most beautiful thing available. If you are a seeker of things antique, here is the most ancient of them all; come and hear, here is the opportunity to own the most unique One!

Satya: *(Shedding tears, going near Krishna}*. I never knew that Narada would do this to me. Please don't listen to him. Refuse to be a plaything in the hands of Narada.

Krishna: *(Sighing deeply, pretending to be miserable)*. My dear, am I free to refuse? You gave me away like a plaything and wish to purchase me back like a plaything. You yourself have given him the right to sell me.

Satya: *(Sobbing)* O Lord, why didn't you tell me all this before? Had you told me that it was wrong to do so, I would never have done it.

Krishna: O Dear, you never asked for my opinion, did you? You told me that you would do this vrata and asked me to be present to be gifted away.

Narada: *(Impatiently)*. Krishna, am I to wait here endlessly for you?

Krishna: *(Hurriedly)* No, no. I am coming.

(Leaves with Narada).

Satya: *(Wiping her tears frantically running here and there)* All of you, hurry up. Bring a huge balance in which the Lord can be weighed. Open the strong room and bring all the gold and silverware. *(People run in all directions).*

(Curtain comes down)

(Scene Three)

(The same scene. There is a huge balance in the centre. Krishna is seated in one pan while the other pan contains several boxes of various sizes. Narada is sitting on a seat. Satyabhama is standing near the balance with a worried look. The pan on which Krishna is seated is lower and the other one is far higher).

Narada: Maharani, all your valuables are over? You haven't got anything else to add?

Satya: *(Wringing her hands)* O sage, I never knew that my Lord is so heavy. I have used up all my valuables and even the immense gold that is yielded by the Syamantakamani. *(A maid brings some new boxes)* Where are these from?

Maid: Maharani, they are from Neela's palace. Neela Devi was very agitated on hearing about the vrata and the weighing. She is also coming.

(Satyabhama becomes pale on hearing this).

Second Maid: *(entering with some more boxes)* Maharani, these are from Devi Nagnajiti's palace. Devi is also coming.

(From different directions the maids bring the boxes and keep them there. Satyabhama keeps all the boxes in the pan but Krishna's side is still lower. Krishna's wives gather around).

Mitravinda: Satyabhama, what is this new vrata in which one's husband is to be given away? I have never heard of such a thing in my life.

Jambavati: Did you think that the Lord is your husband alone? How did you gift him away, without first asking us?

Neela Devi: Did you think that the Lord is some property to be gifted or sold?

(Satyabhama's face is red with shame, anger and sorrow. Anxiously she is putting one box after another in the balance but the pan in which Krishna sits does not rise even by an inch).

Narada: Satyabhama. Only one hour remains for the sun to set. If you can't get Krishna back within this time, then you will have no further chance.

Satya: *(In a tearful voice)* O Divine sage, what should I do now? I have even borrowed the valuables of all the other wives, but the balance still remains lopsided.

Narada: Have you borrowed from Rukmini also? She is not here.

Satya: She doesn't have even half these valuables. How can she help? I did not send word to her.

Narada: She may have something to turn the scales. You never know.

Satya: *(Hopefully)* Do you think so? Let me try. Sundari! *(One maid comes forward)* No, not you. I shall go personally. There is no time to lose through messages. *(Runs out)*

(Curtain drops)

(Scene Four)

(Rukmini's palace. She is seen going round the tulasi plant).

Satya: (Enters in a hurry) Sister, please help me out. I am in a fix and there is no time to lose.

Rukmini: *(Stopping in surprise)* You are in difficulty? How can I help you?

Satya: Sister, in the morning I performed a vrata in which I gifted away the Lord. Sage Narada told me that I could get him back by paying his equal in weight, before the end of the day. I have put all my wealth and borrowed from our sisters, too, but to no avail. Krishna appears to be heavier than all the valuables. There is only one hour before the sun sets. If we are unable to purchase him back today, he will be lost to us forever. Please bring all your valuables and put them in the balance. Who knows it may be the turning point of the scales.

Rukmini: *(Listening to the narration in surprise)* My poor sister! You think you will lose the Lord in another hour? You lost Him, when you thought that He could be gifted away and purchased back. The Lord is not available for such transactions.

Satya: *(Does not understand what she is saying)* Hurry up, sister. There is no time to lose. Get all your valuables.

Rukmini: *(Smiling)* We don't need valuables. *(Plucking a tulasi leaf in a deliberate action)* Come.

(Curtain drops)

(Scene Five)

(Satyabhama's palace with Krishna in the balance. Narada and Krishna's wives are all waiting for Satyabhama 's return).

Satya: *(Entering with Rukmini)* See, sister. This is the position. All our wealth is in the balance. But still the pan is up.

Rukmini: *(Sees the position and smiles)* Sister, please have all the boxes removed from the pan. You can't weigh the Lord against wealth. *(She prostrates to Narada and Krishna).*

(Satyabhama and others quickly remove the boxes, one by one. Going round Krishna with folded

palms, Rukmini, after completing the pradakshina, bows to Krishna and puts the tulasi leaf in the empty pan. Immediately, the pan with the leaf goes down heavily and the pan containing Krishna goes up).

All wives: *(In joy and wonderment cry out)* Sri Krishna ki jai! Rukmini ki jai!

Narada: *(Smiles and takes the tulasi leaf and presses it to his eyes)* Ah, this is the real value of the Lord! Only a real devotee understands the value of the Lord. *(All persons including Narada prostrate to Krishna).*

(Curtain comes down)

Verses To Learn

प्रारभ्यते न खलु विघ्नभयेन नीचैः
प्रारभ्य विघ्नविहता विरमन्ति मध्याः।
विघ्नैः पुनः पुनरपि प्रतिहन्यमानाः
प्रारब्धमुत्तमजना न परित्यजन्ति।।

The weak minded never begin any work for fear of obstacles. Common and ordinary men give up their work, when obstacles block their way. But the very best among men never abandon work, once begun, even if obstructed time and time again.

विद्या नाम नरस्य रूपं अधिकं प्रच्छन्नगुप्तं धनं
विद्या भोगकरी यशःसुखकरी विद्या गुरूणां गुरुः।
विद्या बन्धुजनो विदेशगमने विद्या परं दैवतं
विद्या राजसु पूज्यते न हि धनं विद्याविहीनः पशुः।।

Knowledge is the greatest treasure of man and his most secret and treasured wealth. It confers upon him enjoyment, fame and happiness. Knowledge is the teacher of teachers. Knowledge is one's friend in a foreign country and is the supreme God. Knowledge, and not wealth, is honoured by kings. Truly, a man without knowledge is no better than a beast.

ऐश्वर्यस्य विभूषणं सुजनता शौर्यस्य वाक्संयमः
ज्ञानस्योपशमः श्रुतस्य विनयो वित्तस्य पात्रे व्ययः।
अक्रोधस्तपसः क्षमा प्रभवितुर्धर्मस्य निर्व्याजता
सर्वेषामपि सर्वकारणमिदं शीलं परं भूषणम्।।

Good breeding is the ornament of wealth and power and soft-spokenness is that of valour, self-control and modesty is that of knowledge and learning, proper spending is that of riches, an even temper is that of discipline, mercy is that of kings and honesty is that of dharma. But of all these, the most essential are good manners by far the best ornament of everything!

तृष्णां छिन्धि भज क्षमां जहि मदं पापे रतिं मा कुरु
सत्यं ब्रूह्यनुयाहि साधुपदवीं सेवस्व विद्वज्जनान्।
मान्यान्मानय विद्विषोप्यनुनय प्राच्छादय स्वान्गुणान्
कीर्तिं पालय दुःखिते कुरु दयामेतत्सतां लक्षणम्।।

Keeping away from greed, develop good habits. Give up vanity and temptation to sin. Speak the truth. Follow the path of good men. Serve the learned. Respect those worthy of respect. Be tolerant even to your enemies. Show good manners. Be careful of your reputation and sympathise with the unfortunate. These are the qualities of good men.

CODE OF CONDUCT FOR THE CHINMAYA MISSION MEMBERS

Chinmaya Mission members should:

- Try to live up to and fulfil the motto as well as the pledge of the Mission.
- Daily spare time for meditation and scriptural study.
- Once a week, on a convenient day offer prayers at a nearby temple with members of their family.
- Discover a life of harmony at home and on no account create any domestic unhappiness.
- Have satsang at home with the children and other family members. Reading of the *Ramayana, Mahabharata* and *Bhagavat Mahapurana* in a language familiar to the children would be an important part of the programme.
- Greet other Mission members with 'Hari Om'.
- Inculcate the practice of daily offering pranams to the elders in the house.

Chinmaya Mission Pledge

We stand as one family
bound to each other with love and respect.

We serve as an army
courageous and disciplined,
ever ready to fight against
all low tendencies and false values,
within and without us.

We live honestly
the noble life of sacrifice and service,
producing more than what we consume,
and giving more than what we take.

We seek the Lord's grace
to keep us on the path of virtue, courage and wisdom.

May Thy grace and blessings
flow through us to the world around us.

We believe that the service of our country
is the service of the Lord of Lords,
and devotion to the people
is the devotion to the supreme Self.

We know our responsibilities,
give us the ability and courage
to fulfil them.

Om Tat Sat